Bayerisc
Schlösse
Bavarian A
of State Ca

Nymphenburg

by Elmar D. Schmid

Prestel

Munich · Berlin · London · New York

CONTENTS

opposite page: detail of the decorative plasterwork in the Hall of Mirrors in the Amalienburg

following pages: Nymphenburg Palace, viewed from the park

Franz Anton Bustelli, Nymphenburg porcelain figurines, *c.* 1760, from the Bäuml Porcelain Collection, Nymphenburg Palace

Nymphenburg Palace, situated on the western outskirts of Munich, was the summer residence and seat of Bavaria's electors and kings. Founded in 1664, during the age of absolutism, Nymphenburg was extended on the model of the French royal court to become one of the most extensive palace complexes in Europe. As early as the eighteenth century, not only the palace itself was considered a masterpiece of court art and architecture throughout Europe, but above all its park, designed by French landscape architects, which included the intimate *Pagodenburg, Badenburg, Magdalenenklause* and *Amalienburg* 'pavilions'.

At Nymphenburg, visitors from around the world can still admire the superb works of European art and architecture from the Baroque (the overall complex and the pavilions) and Rococo periods (the Amalienburg and the Great Hall in the palace). The park is an attraction in its own right. A formal French garden laid out in the style of the absolutist era, it was brilliantly redesigned after 1800 as a landscape garden and today is a place where Munich residents go to relax. In addition, magnificent carriages and equestrian equipment once used by the Bavarian rulers are on display in Nymphenburg's *Marstall Museum*, which boasts numerous fine objects used at court in former times.

Of world renown is the *Nymphenburg Porcelain Manufactory* which was housed in the palace as early as the eighteenth century, and which is still in operation within the palace grounds today. An extensive collection of Nymphenburg porcelain (Bäuml Collection) can be admired in the royal stables, complementing the art and cultural-historical aspects of Nymphenburg's palace and museum landscape. In the palace's south crescent is a museum exclusively devoted to the painter *Erwin von Kreibig* (1904–61). Visitors interested in science can spend time in the *Museum of Mankind and Nature*, which is likewise housed in one of the wings, as are many other institutions, among them the headquarters of The Bavarian Administration of State Castles and Palaces.

Richard Wenig, *Ludwig II on a Nocturnal Sleigh Ride, c.* 1885/86,
Marstall Museum, Nymphenburg Palace

The name Nymphenburg is closely asscociated with
the former ruling family, the Wittelsbachs, some of
whose members still live in a wing of the palace. It was
in this palace that Bavaria's 'fairy-tale King', Ludwig II,
was born on 25 August 1845. His ceremonial christen-
ing took place in the Great Hall, and it was at Nymphenburg that he spent much of his youth.

opposite page: Michael Wening, *Nymphenburg Palace,* 1701, copperplate
engraving

In the Baroque and Rococo periods at the Munich court, which was considered one of the most glittering in Europe, the Bavarian Electors (Ferdinand Maria, Maximilian II Emanuel, Karl Albrecht and Maximilian III Joseph) revealed a marked and growing propensity for lavish displays of wealth and power, at the heart of which – besides the *Residenz* in Munich – stood the numerous pleasure palaces around the city. Festivities and celebrations were an integral part of court life at this time and took the form of a *gesamtkunstwerk*, or total work of art. Poetry and theatre, dance and music, hunting and tournaments, fountains and fireworks, architecture and garden design – all paid homage to the ideal and virtuous world of the sovereign.

Nymphenburg Palace owes its foundation as a summer residence to the birth of the long-awaited heir to the throne, Max Emanuel, who was born in 1662 to the Bavarian Elector Ferdinand Maria and his wife, Henriette Adelaide of Savoy, after some ten years of marriage. A site on the edge of the court lands, to the west of the city and the *Residenz*, was chosen for the

François Roëttiers, *Paying Homage to Max Emanuel*, 1717/18, oil on canvas, South Bedroom

new building – a location which, at that time, was still some way out of Munich surrounded by open countryside.

In 1664 construction began to the plans of the north Italian architect Agostino Barelli, who also designed Munich's Theatine Church. Initially, the Italianate 'Nymphenburg summer residence' was a mighty cubic pavilion, flanked by the court church, several outbuildings and a small, walled, geometrical garden. By 1679 the palace complex, in its first incarnation, had nearly been finished.

Nymphenburg Palace acquired its present-day dimensions under the elector Max Emanuel (reigned 1679–1726). Supervised by the court architect Enrico Zuccalli, two off-set pavilions were built on each side of the existing structure, to the north and south. Begun in 1701, the pavilions were linked with the central edifice by galleries. Charles Carbonet, a pupil of Le Nôtre, was commissioned to enlarge the gardens in line with the extended house, laying them out in accordance with the precepts of French garden design.

As Governor of the Spanish Netherlands, the Elector also had a residence in Brussels which, from 1692, enabled him to become better acquainted with developments in the world of art in one of Europe's richest cultural landscapes. When he returned to Munich in 1701, this knowledge was used to the benefit of projects he commissioned in Bavaria.

However, the Spanish War of Succession soon put a stop to construction work because Max Emanuel was again obliged to spend time outside Bavaria, from 1704 to 1715. But this had its positive aspect too, for in exile in Paris he became personally acquainted with the latest trends in French court art, which led him to solicit the services of the architects Germain Boffrand, Alexis Delamair and Robert de Cotte, as well as the landscape architect Claude Desgots, a nephew of Le Nôtre.

When the Elector returned to Munich in 1715, he was accompanied by numerous French, or French-trained, artists. As his palace complexes, such as those in Dachau, Fürstenried, Nymphenburg and Schleissheim, were further enlarged, these artists supplied works conforming to the latest French fashions. Notable among them were the architect Joseph Effner, the landscape architect Dominique Girard, a pupil of Le Nôtre, the sculptor Guillielmus de Grof and the cabinet-maker Johann Adam Pichler. The metalworker Antoine Motté, the painters Nicolas Bertin, Joseph Vivien and François Roëttiers as well as the sculptors Charles Claude Dubut and Giuseppe Volpini also contributed to the decoration of the palaces. Of the fresco painters, the Venetian Jacopo Amigoni was prominent, but local painters, such as the Tyrolean Johann Anton Gumpp, Cosmas Damian Asam, Nikolaus Gottfried Stuber and Balthasar Augustin Albrecht, also received

Maximilian de Geer, *Nymphenburg from the East*, c. 1730, gouache, from the Miniatures' Cabinet in the Residenz, Munich

11

commissions. Veduta paintings were executed by Franz Joachim Beich, Mathias Disel and Maximilian de Geer, while among the stucco workers the Wessobrunn craftsman Johann Baptist Zimmermann was the leading light. So it was that the Munich court developed into one of Europe's foremost centres of the arts.

About 1715, the court architect Joseph Effner, together with the French landscape architect Dominique Girard, designed an overall plan for Nymphenburg and the subsequent extension was carried out in accordance with this plan. Of the measures that were implemented then, the following are the most notable: the central pavilion was redesigned to become the focal point of the ensemble, the royal apartments and living quarters were furnished and decorated, the annexes, situated in front of the main palace, were rebuilt as residences for court officials and the crescent was constructed as an *avant cour* with a circular wall and five pairs of pavilions. Radiating out from the centre, the perspectively off-set structures fused to form a completely symmetrical 'ideal town' which could accommodate the royal household. Included in the design were impressive halls, galleries and apartments, a games tract, an orangery, a theatre auditorium and furniture repository, a palace chapel, an Augustinian convent and church, a monastery and hospice of the Capucin friars, kitchens and butchers' facilities, stables and a dairy, gentlemen's apartments and houses, rooms for artists and craftsmen, the Porcelain Manufactory and a mill.

Overall plan of Nymphenburg, etching, based on a design by François Cuvilliés the Younger, 1772

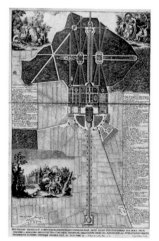

After 1715, and following the plans of Dominique Girard and Joseph Effner, the park was also redesigned and extended, giving it its present dimensions and Baroque style. The central palace area lay on a rectangular island circum-

Bernardo Bellotto, called Canaletto, *Nymphenburg, seen from the Park*, 1761, oil on canvas, in the Residenz, Munich

scribed by canals. The section of the park closest to the palace was to include the Grand Parterre, flanked by bosquets. By way of contrast to these intimate park components, a 'large wood' traversed by paths stretched far beyond the parterre. The main canal, forming the central axis, became the dominating formal element of the park. To the east, a long branch canal, bordered by approach avenues and twenty-six artists' houses, formed an extension of this basic programme. In the transverse axis of the outer park area, two intimate pavilions with their own gardens were erected: the Pagodenburg and the Badenburg. The Magdalenen-klause and, somewhat later, the Amalienburg hunting lodge were added to the wooded areas north and south of the Grand Parterre.

The pavilions were complemented by other intimate components, including two cabinet gardens, a garden in which a ball game was played, a green on which nine-pins was played, an open-air theatre enclosed by hedges and a maze with fountains. Courtiers seeking further diversion could also admire fountains, a cascade and canals whose waters were even plied by gondolas at one time. It all added up to a varied court park in the idiom of the French Regency style. A guidebook of 1792 marvels: "Although the palace at Nymphenburg is very extensive and splendidly decorated on the

inside, nevertheless I make so bold as to say that the park far surpasses it in terms of beauty and good taste. For anyone with eyes to see, the park at Nymphenburg is the finest in all Germany."

Joseph Stephan, *Horse racing at Nymphenburg*, detail, 1779, Marstall Museum

Shortly thereafter, however, the Baroque splendour was to make way for a landscape garden.

Karl Albrecht, first as Elector of Bavaria (reigned 1726–46) and then as Emperor Charles VII (from 1742 onwards), continued the construction work at Nymphenburg begun by his father. He enhanced the complex by adding the palace's crescent. Both palace and crescent were intended to form the centre of a planned 'Carlstadt' ('Charles Town'). His most precious legacy, however, is the Amalienburg in Nymphenburg's park. With this witty, graceful Rococo gem, François Cuvilliés the Elder, a Paris-trained architect, brought Munich court art to its peak of expression. Executed by pre-eminent artists and specialist court workshops, the Amalienburg now ranks among the most charming European architectural creations of the period.

Under Elector Maximilian III Joseph (reigned 1745–77), the Great Hall at Nymphenburg Palace acquired the opulent decoration that can be admired today. Here Johann Baptist Zimmermann, together with François Cuvilliés the Elder, created a major work of Munich court Rococo. The vaulted ceiling of the Palace Chapel was also redesigned. Finally, under Max III Joseph, the Nymphenburg Porcelain Manufactory moved into its present quarters at the front of the palace.

King Max I Joseph of Bavaria, oil on canvas, early 19th century, Marstall Museum

At this time the park, too, was given a new look. The Grand Parterre was remodelled and adorned with statues of the most important gods of Olympus. The exterior flights of steps, also date from this period and have formed a suitably representative entrance to the main building and Great Hall ever since.

Elector Karl Theodor, who ruled in Bavaria and the Palatinate from 1777 to 1799, changed little at Nymphenburg. He had the galleries widened to create new rooms which were furnished in the style of the day. In 1792 Karl Theodor opened the Nymphenburg royal gardens to the public.

When Bavaria became a kingdom, in the early nineteenth century, Nymphenburg resumed its important function as a residential palace. Elector Maximilian IV Joseph, who, as Maximilian I Joseph, was the first King of Bavaria (reigned 1806–25), ordered some of the rooms to be redesigned and appointed with noble Neo-classical furniture. The superintendent of the royal gardens, Friedrich Ludwig Sckell, transformed the geo-metrical French gardens into a landscape garden in the English style. King Maximilian I Joseph died at Nymphenburg in 1825. In subsequent years the palace remained a fa-vourite residence of the Bavarian royal family.

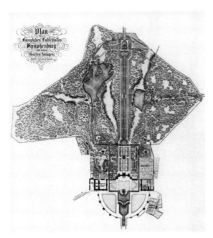

Ludwig Emmert, plan of the royal summer residence at Nymphenburg and its gardens, copperplate engraving, c. 1837

The east façade

Visitors to Nymphenburg Palace arrive at a landscaped crescent which opens up in front of the complex as a large *cour d'honneur*. Water basins and canals, hedged paths and lawns articulate this area in a strict, geometrical fashion. The detached houses along the crescent wall reflect the design principle of the overall palace complex: a loose grouping of pavilions and palace wings in accordance with the laws of perspective, a staggering of structures such that, on approaching the palace, the centre is perceived only gradually, with a symmetry and with coordinated colour schemes that create an impression of coherence. The centre and focal point of the complex is the cubic main pavilion.

To emphasize the fact that this ensemble is the nucleus of the entire palace complex, the façade, designed by Joseph Effner, is adorned with four pilasters which serve to frame the three middle axes. Moreover, all the buildings are arranged in a staggered fashion, much in the manner of the wings on a Baroque stage.

below: the Palace seen from the east

opposite page: the Nymphenburg Porcelain Manufactory pavilion in the crescent

previous pages: the central palace buildings seen from the park

The Great Hall or 'Stone Hall'

The basic features of this central room of the palace complex date from the early days of its construction. It acquired its present-day form under Elector Max Emanuel. At the behest of Elector Max III Joseph, the Great Hall, together with the two halls situated to the front in the west, were remodelled between 1755 and 1757. Aided by François Cuvilliés the Elder, Johann Baptist Zimmermann created his last major work here, a cycle of frescoes, framed by opulent Rococo stucco

The Great Hall or 'Stone Hall' looking to the west with the Garden Room and Musicians' Gallery

work. The result is one of the most accomplished monumental room designs of late Rococo court art in Bavaria.

Alluding to the ruler's duty to secure and maintain peace, the giant ceiling painting depicts the Olympian gods. On the park side, homage is paid to the enthroned water-nymph Flora, a reference to the name Nymphenburg and to horticultural growth.

North Wing

The electors' apartments

This group of rooms to the north of the Great Hall (rooms 2–5) consists of the *First Antechamber* (room 2), the *Second Antechamber* (room 3), the *Former Bedroom* (room 4) and the *North Cabinet* (room 5). Whilst the ceiling paintings date from the time the palace was built, the apartments' other furnishings – both movable and fixed to the wall – were repeatedly modified during the course of some 250 years. Among the furnishings are priceless pieces of eighteenth-century French furniture, such as sets of chairs by Georges Jacob, console tables by Georges Jacob and Adam Weisweiler (rooms 3, 4) and a writing table by G. Jacques Dubois (room 4).

The *First Antechamber* (room 2), with its ceiling depiction of Ceres (Antonio

Zanchi, *c.* 1672), is fitted with sumptuous wall panelling in white with gilt carvings in the Regency style. Modelled on French court art, this magnificent decoration was designed (*c.* 1716/17) in the wake of Max Emanuel's return from Paris. Inset into the panelling are full-figure portraits of Elector Max Emanuel and his second wife, Therese Kunigunde (Joseph Vivien). The *sopraporte* are decorated with allegorical paintings representing the four elements (Jacopo Amigoni).

The ceiling painting in the *Second Antechamber* (room 3) bears the title *Triumph of the Art of War* (Johann Anton Gumpp, 1682). The walls are draped with Baroque tapestries from Brussels. In the middle is Diana, the goddess of hunting, with her retinue, and to the side: garden scenes from a series of pictures of the months.

The Second Antechamber (Gobelin Room) in the North Wing

Peter Jakob Horemans, *The Electoral Families of Bavaria and Saxony Making Music and Playing Cards*, 1761

The *Former Bedroom* (room 4), with its ceiling representation of the sea goddess Thetis (Joseph Werner, 1672/73), contains an historical installation of furniture and paintings, among them *Elector Max Emanuel after the Battle of Harsan* (studio of Joseph Vivien, *c.* 1710) and *Elector Max III Joseph at the Lathe* (Johann Jakob Dorner, 1765). Max Emanuel's *Small Gallery of Beauties* includes portraits of ladies at the court of King Louis XIV of France (Pierre Gobert, *c.* 1715). The painting on the middle wall is particulary striking. It is a court conversation piece showing the electoral families of Bavaria and Saxony making music and playing cards (Peter Jakob Horemans, 1761).

The *North Cabinet* (room 5) was designed by François Cuvilliés the Elder, and features ceiling stucco work by Franz Xaver Feichtmayr the Younger (1763/64). An exquisite roll-top writing table (*c.* 1775–80) graces this intimate room.

Karl Theodor Rooms

Elector Karl Theodor had each of the two Nymphen-
burg galleries widened (1795) by three rooms on the
park side. The furnishings of the north suite of rooms –
Max Emanuel's *Gallery of Beauties* (room 6), the *Coats of
Arms Room* (room 7) and the *Karl Theodor Room* (room
8) – lend the rooms a museum-like quality. Munich
Rococo furniture (room 6) contrasts with pieces from
Paris in the early Neoclassical style (sets of chairs by
Georges Jacob, rooms 6, 7, 8).

Max Emanuel's *Large Gallery of Beauties* (Pierre Gobert,
c. 1715) contains five portraits of ladies at the court
of Louis XIV of France, which adorn the walls of the
room of the same name (room 6). The walls of the
Coats of Arms Room (room 7) are decorated with four
tapestries displaying the joint coat of arms of the
Palatinate/Palatinate-Sulzbach (Savonnerie factory

Heidelberg/Mannheim). Two splendidly framed, full-figure portraits of Elector Karl Theodor and his first wife, Elisabeth Auguste of Pfalz-Sulzbach (Anton Hickel, 1780), dominate the *Karl Theodor Room* (room 8). A portrait of the Elector's second wife, Maria Leopoldine of Austria-Este (Joseph Hauber, 1797), can be seen on the window wall.

North Gallery

The *North Gallery* (room 9), which is a connecting passageway to the electors' former living quarters, is decorated in a classically distinguished style, emulating French Regency court art (*c.* 1717). The walls are adorned with large veduta paintings by Franz Joachim Beich, showing Max Emanuel's palaces, including several views of Nymphenburg, the Fürstenried hunting lodge, Berg Castle on Lake Starnberg and Starnberg Castle, with the electoral fleet on the lake.

South Wing

The apartments of the electors' wives

The impressive rooms south of the Great Hall (rooms 10 to 13) are a mirror image of those to the north and include the *First Antechamber* (room 10), the *Second Antechamber* (room 11), the *Bedroom* (room 12) and the *South Cabinet* (room 13). The ceilings likewise date from the time the palace was built. The décor, which has been changed several times over the centuries, includes exquisite pieces of furniture, such as a richly ornamented Baroque table with a pietra dura mosaic top (Florence, room 11), two commodes by Bernard II Vanrisamburgh (Paris, *c.* 1731–33, room 11), a writing table with a Japanese lacquer front (Paris, *c.* 1731–33, room 13) and a bureau by Jean-Baptiste Saunier and Christophe Wolff (Paris, *c.* 1760, room 12).

The *First Antechamber* (room 10) contains a ceiling painting of the water-nymph Arethusa, the goddess of Syracuse (Antonio Domenico Triva, 1673), and wall

The Bedroom in the South Wing, with a ceiling painting of the goddess Flora, *c.* 1675

panelling in the Rococo style. The room's main decoration comprises two full-figure portraits of Karl Albrecht and his wife, Maria Amalia (George Desmarées, *c.* 1766). The imperial couple are depicted with the insignia of office.

The ceiling painting in the *Second Antechamber* (room 11) depicts Cybele, the earth goddess. The room is draped with red damask, and on its side walls there are two large paintings showing the electoral family in the guise of figures from Classical mythology (Stefano Catani, *c.* 1674). Thus Elector Ferdinand Maria appears as King Endymion and his wife, Henriette Adelaide, as the goddess Diana, portrayed together with their childen. On the

The *secrétaire en armoire* in the Bedroom, Jean Baptiste Saunier/ Christophe Wolff, Paris, *c.* 1760

middle wall there is a double portrait of the same electoral pair (Sebastiano Bombelli, 1666). The magnificent splendour of the Munich court at the time of the palace's construction is reflected not least of all in their exquisitely fashionable clothing.

The *Bedroom* (room 12) is dominated by a ceiling painting of the goddess Flora. Its walls are hung with green damask which matches the colour of the richly decorated Baroque bed canopy. The child portrait (Sebastiano Bombelli, 1666) of Max Emanuel and his sister Maria Anna Christina, his elder by two years, both dressed in the latest French fashions, is a particularly endearing contribution to court portraiture of the period. The wall next to the bed baldachin displays a pair of matching Baroque portraits, showing Elector Max Emanuel and his second wife, Therese Kunigunde (Johann Adreas Wolff, 1704). The allegorical painting above the fireplace pays homage to Max Emanuel on the occasion of his return from exile in Paris (François Roëttier, 1717/18).

The Chinese Lacquer Cabinet, detail of the carved lacquer wall panels

The *South Cabinet* (room 13), or Chinese Lacquer Cabinet, was remodelled in 1763/64 by François Cuvilliés the Elder, Franz Xaver Feichtmayr (stucco work) and Johann Georg Hörringer (lacquer paintings). The East-Asian, carved lacquer wall panels give the little room an exotic character.

South Gallery (room 14)

The connecting passageway leading to the apartments of the electors' wives was not hung as an intimate picture gallery until about 1760. It houses ten veduta paintings depicting the electoral palaces of Schleissheim, Lustheim, Dachau, Lichtenberg, Haag, Kling, Trausnitz in Landshut and Isareck (Franz Joachim Beich, Nikolaus Gottfried Stuber, Joseph Stephan).

South Pavilion

From the time of Elector Max Emanuel onwards, the main floor of the inner South Pavilion (rooms 15–20) housed the apartments of the wives of the electors and, later, the Bavarian Queens. It achieved its present form when it was rebuilt from 1806 to 1810 for Queen Caroline, the second wife of King Max I Joseph. The chambers – *Former Dining Room* (room 15), *Maserzimmer* (room 16), *Blue Salon* (room 19) and *Bedroom* (room 20)

The Bedroom in the
South Pavilion where King
Ludwig II was born

right: round table,
Paris, *c*. 1800/05,
in the Blue Salon

Johann Halbig, *Crown Prince Ludwig and Prince Otto*, 1850, in the Bedroom in the South Pavilion

– are decorated in a simple, yet refined, Neoclassical style.

Except for the former dining room, the Queen's Apartments have retained their original furniture, revealing the French-influenced décor favoured by the Munich court at the time. A particularly magnificent piece is the round table (Paris, *c.* 1800) with its polychrome veneering in exotic precious woods and bronzes in the form of Pharaohs' heads (room 19). The *Bedroom* (room 20) is where King Ludwig II, Bavaria's 'fairy-tale King', was born on 25 August 1845.

Today the Queen's *Former Dining Room* (room 15) accommodates King Ludwig I's *Gallery of Beauties*, a world-famous series of portraits of beautiful women painted to a commission from the King by Joseph Stieler for the Munich *Residenz*. The paintings, executed between 1827 and 1850, reflect Ludwig I's ideal of beauty rather than the social rank of the sitters. Royal princesses and humble Munich burghers' daughters, such as Helene Sedlmayr, whose father was a cobbler, are accorded equal value in the series. Romanticism and Biedermeier, and not least the King's predilection for such southern countries as Italy and Greece, can be seen in these likenesses of comely maidens and young women.

Joseph Stieler, *Anna Hillmayer*, 1829, in the Gallery of Beauties

Coat of arms showing the union between Bavaria and Poland, above the altar in the Palace Chapel

Palace Chapel

Hidden away in the North Pavilion is the *Palace Chapel* (room 21), which was begun in 1702, under Elector Max Emanuel, by Antonio Viscardi after a design by Enrico Zuccalli. Political events, however, delayed its construction until Joseph Effner was able to complete the chapel after 1715. The grand Baroque high altar incorporates an older group of figures – Christ and Mary Magdalene. The dynamic, late Rococo vaulting and the frescoes depicting the life of Mary Magdalene (Joseph Mölck, 1759) introduce a cheerful note into the classically austere chapel.

right: the interior of the Palace Chapel

following pages: the Monopteros on Badenburg Lake, Leo von Klenze, 1862/65

Dominique Girard and Joseph Effner drew up their much-admired plan for Nymphenburg around 1715, on the basis of which the walled palace park was also laid out in its present dimensions. The park contains a number of residences which may variously be described as small palaces, large garden pavilions or lodges. Conceived as focal points of interest for the park components related to them, they include the Pagodenburg (1716–19), the Badenburg (1718–22), the Magdalenenklause (1725–28) and the Amalienburg hunting lodge (1734–39). Of the geometrically designed French park, the canal system has survived as well as the articulation of the area in front of the palace and the Grand Parterre behind it, the latter being bordered with statues of Greek gods and vases from the second half of the eighteenth century (by Giovanni Marchiori, Johann Baptist Straub, Ignaz Günther, Dominikus Auliczek and Roman Anton Boos). Something else that still exists today is the great marble cascade, located at the point where the main canal enters the palace grounds, with its rich statuary (Giuseppe Volpini, de Grof, both father and son, Ignaz Günther and Roman Anton Boos). Besides the garden pavilions with their ancillary structures, several individual buildings likewise date from the time the formal Baroque park was laid out, such as the aviary in the South Cabinet Garden (François Cuvilliés the Elder, 1751–57) and the Pump House, next to which stands a picturesque group of cottages ('The Hamlet').

About 1800, during the rule of Elector Max IV Joseph, who, in 1806, became the first Bavarian King, work was begun on generally remodelling

right: the Grand Parterre

opposite page, top: the Baroque marble cascade

Nymphenburg park as a 'natural' landscape garden in the English style. The brilliant landscape architect Friedrich Ludwig Sckell was commissioned to plan and execute the transformation. By the time the king died in 1825, work had largely been finished. Retaining the geometrical elements (the Grand Parterre and main canal), Sckell redesigned the extensive lateral wooded areas between the Badenburg and the Amalienburg, and between the Pagodenburg and the Magdalenen-

klause. Making use of meadows that lay between the gentle undulations of the terrain which were fringed by the animated outline of the edges of the woodland, and utilizing lakes with variously landscaped banks as well as a multiplicity of meandering paths, Sckell created a severe Neoclassical landscape garden which had as its ideal a pure, sublime image of nature. He avoided introducing new buildings, adding only the Summer Pavilion in the small Prince's Garden (c. 1800), the Monopteros (Leo von Klenze and Carl Mühlthaler, 1862–65) on Badenburg Lake and three hothouses near the Grand Parterre. He incorporated new highlights in the form of individual garden sculptures (the Pan group near the Badenburg) and the magnificent fountains both in front of and behind the palace. Viewed as a whole, Sckell's layout of Nymphenburg park may be claimed to be "one of the most brilliant ever produced in landscape garden design" (F. Hallbaum).

The Pagodenburg

The Pagodenburg was built between 1716 and 1719 by Joseph Effner to a commission from Elector Max Emanuel. Sited north of the main canal, it respects the original plan of the park. To the south of the little palace lies a garden parterre, and to the north a green where the 'Mailspiel', a game similar to golf, was played. A contemporary account reports: "This Indian building is a place where the lords and ladies rest after the exertions of a round of 'Mailspiel' ... The lower floor houses a hall and two cabinets, and the panelling has been executed in Arab and Indian styles with all manner of Chinese figures and pagodas."

The pavilion is constructed around a central octagon, extended on four sides by almost square projecting structures, lending it a cruciform shape. The two-storey edifice has round-arched windows and doorways on the ground floor and segmental-arched windows to

The Pagodenburg, seen from the south

the upper storey. It is articulated vertically by colossal Corinthian pilasters which also serve to frame the various structural elements.

The octagonal structure is readily discernible in the *Hall* on the ground floor (room 1) because every side of the octagon has the same wall articulation. The colours blue and white predominate which, together with the exotic elements of the partly ornamental, partly figural ceiling painting and the Dutch tiles, allude to China and porcelain production. The upper floor accommo-

The Pagodenburg, the Boudoir

dates very small but cleverly designed rooms. The *Chinese Drawing Room* (room 2) with Chinese wallpaper and black-grounded lacquer painting looks exotic thanks to its colour scheme. The *Chinese Cabinet* (room 3), by contrast, has red-based lacquerwork. Despite its European Regency-style decoration, the *Boudoir* (room 4) also has an exotic air on account of its bizarre shape. The rooms were furnished by Johann Anton Gumpp and Johann Adam Pichler. The Pagodenburg is a prime example of eighteenth-century chinoiserie which was very much in vogue at the time.

For his interiors, Joseph Effner designed not only the permanent fixtures but also the furniture. Generally speaking, he drew on the formal vocabulary of the French Regency style. However, in particular instances, he developed new ideas of his own. Thus, in the case of the rooms in the Pagodenburg, he introduced exotic

right: the Chinese Drawing Room

below: the Chinese Cabinet Room

elements into the furniture, creating unique decorative items, such as candlesticks with dragons' heads. Priceless individual pieces complete the exquisite furnishings, such as a games table (Paris, *c.* 1720/25) and two small Japanese lacquer cabinets remodelled as commodes (Paris, *c.* 1715/20).

Lacquer commode, Japan and France, *c.* 1715/20, in the Chinese Cabinet

The Badenburg

Extolling the Badenburg, Pierre de Bretagne, who was Max Emanuel's father confessor, said: "The house of baths is a veritable artistic masterpiece." The park pavilion was built between 1718 and 1722 according to plans by Joseph Effner, and stands as the central feature of the southern half of the park in its own garden area. Taking up 'bathing' as the theme of this *maison de plaisance*, Effner created a unique *gesamtkunstwerk*.

The Badenburg, the Banqueting Hall

left: the Badenburg, viewed from the north

The ground plan of the main floor consists of an oblong hall with rounded corners. Adjoining it to the south is a similarly oblong wing, including the *Bath* (room 3) and the *Electors' Apartments* (Antechamber, Bedroom, Cabinet, Dressing Room — rooms 2, 4, 5, 6). While the *Banqueting Hall* (room 1)

The Bath with viewing gallery

takes up two storeys, the space
above the apartments in the
south annex houses small, com-
fortable rooms (destroyed in
1944). The basement accommodates the bath itself, the heating
room, a kitchen and additional
bathing rooms.

The façade of the *Banqueting
Hall* is set off with round-arched
windows and doorways, above
which oval windows are arranged
lengthwise, and huge pilasters. By
contrast, the two-storey south
façade, which has a double row
of rectangular doors and windows, is restrained and relatively
unadorned.

The hall itself boasts some
magnificent stucco work (Charles
Claude Dubut) and ceiling frescoes (Jacopo Amigoni, destroyed
in 1944, subsequently restored).
Its pictorial programme relates to
the element of water, drawing on
Classical mythology. The bath is
also sumptuously decorated with
Dutch tiling to the lower area
and scagliola plates to the upper,
with a gallery and a ceiling painting depicting fountain motifs
(Nicolas Bertin). The *Electors'
Apartments* are fitted with wall
panelling, mirror ornaments and

a ceiling painted with monkey scenes, but are particularly notable for the Chinese wallpaper in each of the four rooms.

As a bathing pavilion, the Badenburg belongs to a long tradition dating back to the opulent baths of the Roman emperors while also including elements of the Islamic bathing culture. Although conceptually indebted to Baroque baths, Effner's bathing pavilion represents a new creation which was both admired and imitated (Bonn, Kassel, Schwetzingen). Contemporary reports consistently eulogized the Badenburg. A travel account of 1792, for example, warns that no visit to Nymphenburg should omit either of two things: "One is the Amalienburg ... , the other, in a different corner of the park and built by Elector Maximilian Emanuel, are the finest baths imaginable, splendidly equipped with all conveniences. I do not recall seeing anything more delicate or better thought-out anywhere. The pool is so large that one can comfortably swim in it, and if there are people who just want to watch, there is a place (the gallery) where they can position themselves and look on."

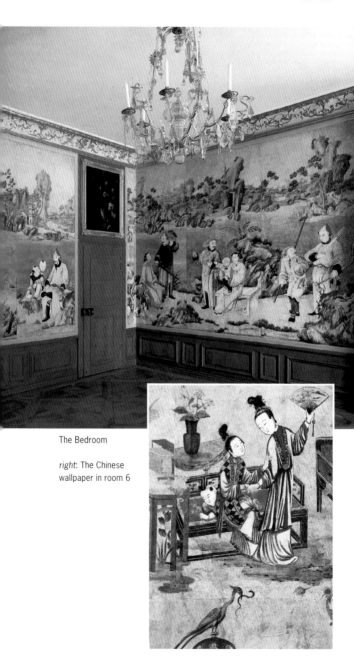

The Bedroom

right: The Chinese
wallpaper in room 6

The Magdalenenklause

The third pavilion in the palace grounds, built by Joseph Effner, is the Magdalenenklause (Magdalene Hermitage), sited north of the Grand Parterre and constructed between 1725 and 1728. Elector Max Emanuel did not live to see the completion of the building, which was finished by his son, Elector Karl Albrecht.

The Magdalenenklause was conceived as the living quarters of a hermit and stands in a small, 'overgrown'

The Mag-
dalenen-
klause,
viewed
from the
south

wood. Built with tiles and partly plastered, it looks like a ruin from the outside. Cracks in the masonry and crumbling plaster serve as a reminder of the frailty of all things earthly.

The one-storey building has a rectangular ground plan and is extended to the south and north with semi-circular conchae. At the corners of the east front are circular turrets. The south part of the Hermitage comprises the *Grotto Chapel of St. Mary Magdalene* (room 2) and a similarly grottoed *Entrance Hall* (room 1). To the

The chancel in the Grotto Chapel

Byzantine crucifix in
the refectory

north are the *Electors'
Apartments (*rooms
3–6), which consist
of monastically
austere rooms with
oak panelling 'à la
Capucine' and dec-
orated with copper
engravings. Individual furnishings emphasize the
building's strangeness, including the altarpiece in the
chapel with a crucifix and two candlesticks made from
a narwhal tusk and a Byzantine table crucifix in the
refectory, which Max Emanuel took as booty during
the Turkish wars in Hungary.

The hermitage enabled the Elector to escape from
reality, although his genuine contemplation here was
mixed with courtly play. It is another extraordinary
Effner creation. By using exotic and historicizing
architectural forms, he produced a strange, romantic,
anachronistic structure that incorporates both a
serious aspect and
elements of the court-
ly art of metamor-
phosis.

Death (The Last Four Things),
wax relief, southern Germany,
early 18th century, Prayer
Room

The Amalienburg

In 1734 Elector Karl Albrecht ordered work to commence on the Amalienburg, a small pleasure palace and hunting lodge for his wife, Maria Amalia, a daughter of Emperor Joseph I. Sited opposite the Magdalenenklause, the building, which was completed in 1739, was conceived as a small independent palace complex.

The Amalienburg, the garden front, viewed from the east

François Cuvilliés the Elder supplied the designs for the architecture and decoration, and was responsible for overseeing the craftsmen involved. The stucco work was largely done by Johann Baptist Zimmermann, the woodcarving by Johann Joachim Dietrich and the painting by Joseph Pasqualin Moretti.

This outwardly simple, yet noble, building, whose central section is slightly accentuated by a flat dome

left: detail of the ornate plaster ceiling above the hollow moulding in the Hall of Mirrors

The Hall of Mirrors

right: detail of the ornately carved panelling in the Bedroom

The Bedroom or Yellow Room

with a platform, houses a suite of rooms of striking unity. At the same time, however, the individual rooms are differentiated according to the precepts of French court art and in each case variously designed with great refinement.

The *Large Salon*, or *Hall of Mirrors* (room 5), forms the centre of the pavilion. The *Blue Cabinet* and the *Yellow Room*, or *Bedroom* (room 4), adjoin to the south, whilst the *Hunting Room* (room 6) and the *Indian Cabinet*, or *Pheasant Room* (room 7), abut to the north. The abbreviated wing structures accommodate the *Dressing Room*, the *Dog and Gun Room*, the *Retirade* and the *Kitchen*.

The richness of the decoration increases towards the centre, culminating in the *Hall of Mirrors*, a circular room with a flat dome. In this hall, detailing of the stucco work executed by Johann Baptist Zimmermann is less prominent. Silver, off white and delicate blue are the dominant colours. The alternation of windows, mirrors and doors, and the interplay of real and reflected light, seem to remove the room's borders, so that one feels as if one has been transposed into an open pavilion, half arbour, half grotto, above which is the firmament seen through the dome.

Like the Hall of Mirrors, the *Bedroom*, or *Yellow Room*, is also richly decorated. The wall carvings, painted silver on a lemon-coloured ground, combine with the delicate blue stucco work which extends beyond the white ceiling, to form a graceful, rhythmically animated 'weave'. The wall panelling, executed by the court woodcarver Johann Joachim Dietrich, is one of the finest examples of court carving of the period. The bed niche is flanked by two portraits. The one on the left shows Elector Karl Albrecht, who commissioned the Amalienburg, while the one on the right portrays Maria Amalia, for whom the 'hunting lodge' was built. Both are in hunting attire.

The *Hunting Room*, a pendant to the Bedroom, is decorated as a small picture salon, in which the paintings – in the Rococo manner – are incorporated into the wall decoration, painted silver on a straw-coloured

The Elector's wife, Maria Amalie, Dressed in Hunting Attire, oil on canvas, from the studio of George Desmarées, the Bedroom, Amalienburg

background and arranged in two rows, one above the other. Particularly charming are the depictions painted by Peter Jakob Horemans of court hunts and festivities held by the electoral couple and their retinue.

The *Pheasant Room*, or *Indian Cabinet*, has an exotic atmosphere. Its walls are embellished with linen that is painted and waxed in the manner of Chinese wallpaper. The pheasant motif is a reference to the Pheasant Garden, which was laid out in 1734 near the Amalienburg. The *Dog and Gun Room* contains paintings of hunting scenes and hunting trophies, executed in the Indian manner in blue on a white background.

The *Kitchen*, too, is a remarkable creation with an exotic air. Whilst the blue-and-white ceiling is painted with Chinese scenes, the walls are decorated with Dutch tiles. The highlights of this unusually imaginative and colourful tiling are the flower vases and Chinese scenes.

The Amalienburg is one of the most exquisite creations in the European Rococo style. Its ground plan, exterior and sequence of rooms form a *gesamtkunstwerk* of rare beauty. During his student days in Paris from 1720 to 1724, François Cuvilliés the Elder became acquainted with the art of the French metropolis. Drawing on the knowledge and skills he acquired there, this brilliant architect designed the Amalienburg, truly one of his most outstanding works.

following pages: Dutch tiling and ceramic pictures in the kitchen

Front cover: Nymphenburg Palace, viewed from the park
Back cover: The Great Hall in the palace; the Badenburg, viewed
from the north

© content and layout: Prestel Verlag,
Munich · Berlin · London · New York, 2005

Photographic credits: all pictures are from the archives held at the
Bavarian Administration of State Castles, Palaces, Gardens, and
Lakes (incl. photos by Maria Custodis, Tanja Mayr and Rainer
Herrmann), with the exception of pp. 19, 48/49: Kerstin von
Zabuesnig, Starnberg; p. 20: Achim Bunz, Munich; pp. 16/17:
ambild, Finsing; p. 22: K. Rainer, Salzburg

Prestel's **'Museum Guide Compact'** series, covering Bavaria's
castles, palaces, gardens and lakes, is published in cooperation
with the Bavarian Authority for State Castles and Palaces, edited by
Peter O. Krückmann

The Deutsche Bibliothek holds a record of this publication in the
Deutsche Nationalbibliographie; detailed bibliographical data can be
found under: http://dnb.ddb.de

Prestel Verlag
Königinstr. 9 · D–80539 Munich
Tel. (089) 381709-0, Fax (089) 381709-35;
4 Bloomsbury Place · London WC1A 2QA
Tel. (020) 7323 5004, Fax (020) 7636 8004;
900 Broadway, Suite 603 · New York, NY 10003
Tel. (212) 995-2720, Fax (212) 995-2733

Translated from the German by Christian Godden
Edited by Michele Schons

Editorial direction: Christopher Wynne

Design: Rainald Schwarz, Munich
Typesetting: Bernd Hüller, Munich
Lithography: ReproLine, Munich
Printing: Peradruck, Gräfelfing
Binding: Attenberger, Munich

Printed in Germany on acid-free paper

ISBN 3-7913-2370-9 (English edition)
ISBN 3-7913-2373-3 (German edition)